Ms McCulloch

BOOK 3

Prim-Ed
Publishing
www.prim-ed.com

Grammar minutes

100 minutes to practise and reinforce essential skills

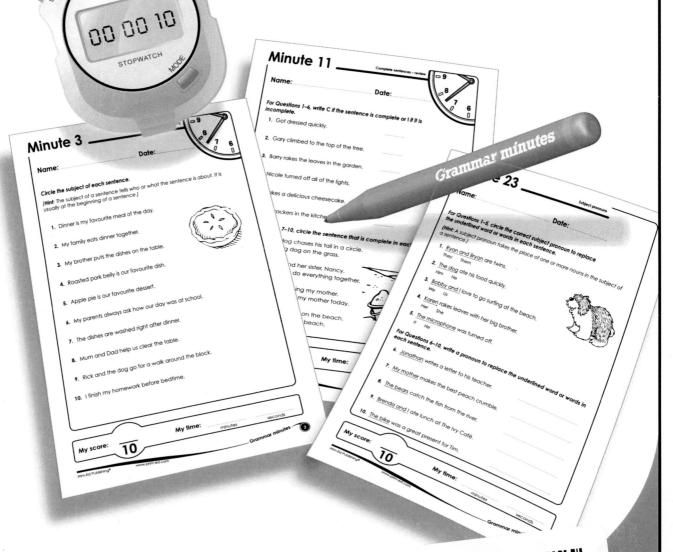

Carmen S Jones

6329

57/6

Grammar minutes *Book 3*

Published by Prim-Ed Publishing® 2011 under licence to Creative Teaching Press.
Copyright© 2005 Creative Teaching Press.
This version copyright© Prim-Ed Publishing® 2011

ISBN 978-1-84654-296-1
PR–6329

Titles available in this series:

Grammar minutes Book 1
Grammar minutes Book 2
Grammar minutes Book 3
Grammar minutes Book 4
Grammar minutes Book 5
Grammar minutes Book 6

Internet websites
In some cases, websites or specific URLs may be recommended. While these are checked and rechecked at the time of publication, the publisher has no control over any subsequent changes which may be made to webpages. It is *strongly* recommended that the class teacher checks *all* URLs before allowing pupils to access them.

View all pages online

Website: www.prim-ed.com

GRAMMAR MINUTES – BOOK 3

Foreword

Grammar minutes is a six-book series for primary school pupils that provides a structured daily programme of easy-to-follow activities in grammar. The main objective is grammar proficiency, attained by teaching pupils to apply grammar skills to answer questions effortlessly and rapidly. The questions in this book provide pupils with practice in the following key areas of grammar instruction:

- *sentence structure*
- *verbs*
- *adjectives*
- *compound words*
- *articles*
- *nouns*
- *pronouns*
- *adverbs*
- *contractions*
- *prepositions.*

Grammar minutes – Book 3 features 100 'minutes', each with 10 classroom-tested problems. Use this comprehensive resource to improve your pupils' overall grammar proficiency, which will promote greater self-confidence in their grammar skills as well as provide the everyday practice necessary to succeed in testing situations. Designed to be implemented in numerical order from 1 to 100, the activities in *Grammar minutes* are developmental through each book and across the series.

Comprehensive teachers notes, record-keeping charts, a scope-and-sequence table (showing when each new concept and skill is introduced) and photocopiable pupil reference materials are also included.

How many minutes does it take to complete a 'grammar minute'?

Pupils will enjoy challenging themselves as they apply their grammar knowledge and understanding to complete a 'grammar minute' in the fastest possible time.

Titles available in this series:

- *Grammar minutes – Book 1*
- *Grammar minutes – Book 2*
- *Grammar minutes – Book 3*
- *Grammar minutes – Book 4*
- *Grammar minutes – Book 5*
- *Grammar minutes – Book 6*

Contents

Teachers notes

How to use this book

Grammar minutes can be used in a variety of ways, such as:

- **a speed test.** As the teacher starts a stopwatch, pupils begin the 'minute'. As each pupil finishes, he/she raises a hand and the teacher calls out the time. The pupil records this time on the appropriate place on the sheet. Alternatively, a particular time can be allocated for the whole class to complete the 'minute' in.
  Pupils record their scores and time on their 'minute journal' (see page vii).

- **a whole-class activity.** Work through the 'minute' together as a teaching or reviewing activity.

- **a warm-up activity.** Use a 'minute' a day as a 'starter' or warm-up activity before the main part of the lesson begins.

- **a homework activity.** If given as a homework activity, it would be most beneficial for the pupils if the 'minute' is corrected and reviewed at the start of the following lesson.

Grammar minutes strategies

Encourage pupils to apply the following strategies to help improve their scores and decrease the time taken to complete the 10 questions.

- To use strategies whenever possible.
- To move quickly down the page, answering the problems they know first.
- To come back to problems they are unsure of, after they have completed all other problems.
- To make educated guesses when they encounter problems they are not familiar with.

A *Grammar minute* pupil activity page.

Name and date
Pupils write their name and the date in the spaces provided.

Questions
There are 10 problems, providing practice in every key area of grammar proficiency.

Score
Pupils record their score out of 10 in the space provided.

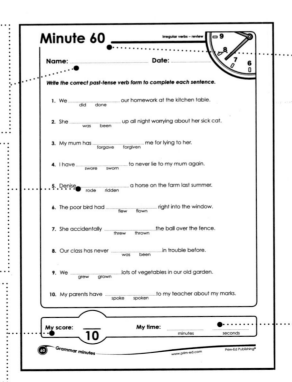

'Grammar minute' number
Grammar minutes are designed to be completed in numerical order.

Time
Pupils record the time taken to complete the 'minute' at the bottom of the sheet. (This is optional.)

Prim-Ed Publishing®
www.prim-ed.com

Teachers notes

Marking

Answers are provided for all activities. How these activities are marked will vary according to the teacher's organisational policy. Methods could include whole-class checking, partner checking, individual pupil checking or collection by the teacher.

Diagnosis of problem areas

Grammar minutes provides the teacher with immediate feedback of whole-class and individual pupil understanding. This information is useful for future programming and planning of further opportunities to practise and review the skills and concepts which need addressing.

Make use of the structured nature of the questions to diagnose problem areas; rather than asking who got 10 out of 10, ask the pupils who got Question 1 correct to raise their hands, Question 2, Question 3 etc. In this way, you will be able to quickly determine which concepts are causing problems for the majority of the pupils. Once the routine of *Grammar minutes* is established, the teacher will have time to work with individuals or small groups to assist them with any areas causing problems.

Meeting the needs of individuals

The structure of *Grammar minutes* allows some latitude in the way the books are used; for example, it may be impractical (as well as demoralising for some) for all pupils to be using the same book. It can also be difficult for teachers to manage the range of abilities found in any one classroom, so while pupils may be working at different levels from different books, the familiar structure makes it easier to cope with individual differences. An outline of the suggested age range levels each book is suited to is given on page iii.

Additional resources:

- **Minute records**

  Teachers can record pupil scores and times on the **Minute records** table located on page vi.

- **Scope and sequence**

  The **Scope-and-sequence table** gives the 'minute' in which each new skill and concept appears for the first time.

- **Minute journal**

  Once a 'minute' is completed, pupils record their score and time on their **Minute journal**, located on page vii.

- **Answers to all questions are found on pages 101 to 105.**

Minute records

Pupil's name: .... Class: ....

Minute:	Date	Score	Time	Minute:	Date	Score	Time	Minute:	Date	Score	Time	Minute:	Date	Score	Time
1				26				51				76			
2				27				52				77			
3				28				53				78			
4				29				54				79			
5				30				55				80			
6				31				56				81			
7				32				57				82			
8				33				58				83			
9				34				59				84			
10				35				60				85			
11				36				61				86			
12				37				62				87			
13				38				63				88			
14				39				64				89			
15				40				65				90			
16				41				66				91			
17				42				67				92			
18				43				68				93			
19				44				69				94			
20				45				70				95			
21				46				71				96			
22				47				72				97			
23				48				73				98			
24				49				74				99			
25				50				75				100			

Notes:

....

....

....

....

www.prim-ed.com   Prim-Ed Publishing®

Minute journal

Name: ....

Minute	Date	Score	Time

Minute	Date	Score	Time

Things I am good at.

• ....

• ....

Things I need to work on.

• ....

• ....

Things I am good at.

• ....

• ....

Things I need to work on.

• ....

• ....

SCOPE-AND-SEQUENCE TABLE BOOK 3

www.prim-ed.com Prim-Ed Publishing®

Minute 1

Name: .... **Date:** ....

Write C if the sentence is complete or I if it is incomplete.

(**Hint**: Remember that a complete sentence is a group of words that tells a complete thought.)

1. The jugglers at the school fair. ....

2. You should stretch before you exercise. ....

3. The train ride from Mount Snowdon. ....

4. The lazy dog. ....

5. The bee flew from flower to flower. ....

6. My favourite story is 'Hansel and Gretel'. ....

7. The animals in the Arctic. ....

8. Jenny bought purple gloves for winter. ....

9. Regina paints pictures of animals. ....

10. My house during the storm. ....

My score: $\dfrac{}{10}$

My time: ....
minutes   seconds

Minute 2

Name: .... **Date:** ....

For Questions 1–7, write Yes *if the sentence is in the correct word order or* No *if it is not.*

1. My dad is building a tree house for me.   ....

2. The puppy around ran the house.   ....

3. I watching television am.   ....

4. Maggie taught her dog a new trick.   ....

5. The woman waited on the bench.   ....

6. The flowers had a sweet smell.   ....

7. The tent is for our camping trip.   ....

For Questions 8–10, rewrite the sentences in the correct word order.

(**Hint**: *Remember that a sentence must begin with a capital letter.*)

8. ....
   we have quiet to be library in the.

9. ....
   writing the pupils are letters.

10. ....
    Christopher Columbus about I reading am.

My score: _____
10

My time: ....
   minutes   seconds

Name: .... **Date:** ....

Circle the subject of each sentence.

*(**Hint**: The subject of a sentence tells who or what the sentence is about. It is usually at the beginning of a sentence.)*

1. Dinner is my favourite meal of the day.

2. My family eats dinner together.

3. My brother puts the dishes on the table.

4. Roasted pork belly is our favourite dish.

5. Apple pie is our favourite dessert.

6. My parents always ask how our day was at school.

7. The dishes are washed right after dinner.

8. Mum and Dad help us clear the table.

9. Rick and the dog go for a walk around the block.

10. I finish my homework before bedtime.

My score: $\dfrac{}{10}$

My time: ....
  minutes   seconds

Minute 4

Name: .... **Date:** ....

Circle the predicate of each sentence.

*(**Hint**: The predicate of a sentence tells what someone or something is or does. It is usually the last part of a sentence.)*

1. Tracy bought a gift for the party.

2. The strong wind blew my scarf away.

3. The sleeping tiger did not see the deer.

4. Mrs Smith runs six kilometres every morning.

5. Grace went to the theatre.

6. We made a sundae with vanilla ice-cream.

7. The squirrel put the nuts in its mouth.

8. My big sister is excited about getting a car.

9. Felicity and Lucy go hiking at Spring Park.

10. Josh works on his science project at the library.

My score: $\dfrac{\quad\quad}{10}$ **My time:** ....
minutes   seconds

Minute 5

Name: .... **Date:** ....

For Questions 1–5, circle the subject of each sentence.

1. Rachel made enough cupcakes for everyone.

2. Melinda and Claudia are my best friends.

3. Mrs Lee's party lasted for three hours.

4. My mother was angry that I did not clean my room.

5. My friend, Ashley, helped her dad wash their cars.

For Questions 6–10, circle the predicate of each sentence.

6. I am taking guitar lessons from Mr Verlaine.

7. Ralph had a piñata at his birthday party.

8. The loud cricket was chirping outside my window.

9. Lao was excited to go skateboarding with his friends.

10. David felt sick after eating three hamburgers.

My score: ──── / 10

My time: ....
minutes   seconds

Name: .... **Date:** ....

For Questions 1–7, write Yes if the sentence is a declarative sentence or No if it is not.

(Hint: A declarative sentence is a statement that tells something.)

1. Toby feeds the turtles in the lake. ....

2. Fran picks the apples off the trees. ....

3. Why are we not going to the park today? ....

4. It snows in April in some parts of the world. ....

5. Why do the birds fly south for the winter? ....

6. Wow, that watermelon is huge! ....

7. We have lots of books about dinosaurs. ....

For Questions 8–10, answer each question with a declarative sentence.

8. ....
   What is your name?

9. ....
   Where do you live?

10. ....
    How old are you?

My score:

$\overline{}$
10

My time:

....
minutes seconds

Minute 7

Name: .... **Date:** ....

For Questions 1–6, write Yes if the sentence is an interrogative sentence or No if it is not.

*(**Hint:** An interrogative sentence is a question.)*

1. Are we going to Italy this summer? ....

2. Our new neighbours are very nice people. ....

3. How did you do on your science test? ....

4. Why isn't Janet going with us to the museum? ....

5. May I please have another slice of cherry tart? ....

6. I am going to write a letter to my grandmother. ....

For Questions 7–10, circle the correct interrogative sentence in each pair.

7. (a) How are you?
   (b) I am fine?

8. (a) I am going to the shop?
   (b) Where are you going?

9. (a) I like to play netball?
   (b) What do you like to do?

10. (a) Who is your teacher?
    (b) My teacher is Ms Martins?

My score: ___
       10

My time: ....
          minutes   seconds

Minute 8

Name: .... **Date:** ....

Write Yes *if the sentence is an exclamatory sentence or* No *if it is not.*

*(**Hint**: An exclamatory sentence shows strong feelings.)*

1. Wow, he can really run fast!   ....

2. That was the best film I ever saw!   ....

3. Susan washes her hair with baby shampoo.   ....

4. I got all the answers right on the test!   ....

5. There's a mouse in the kitchen!   ....

6. Will you sweep under the table?   ....

7. The boys are at a rugby match.   ....

8. Watch out for that snake in the grass!   ....

9. Joel lives on Hermit Street in Roxby Downs.   ....

10. You really saved my life!   ....

My score: ___
    10

My time: ....
                    minutes   seconds

Minute 9

Name: .... Date: ....

For Questions 1–6, write Yes *if the sentence is an imperative sentence* or No *if it is not.*

*(**Hint**: An imperative sentence is a command. It ends with a full stop.)*

1. Don't run into the street. ....

2. I can speak English and Japanese. ....

3. Get off the bed before you fall. ....

4. Michael is going to clean the board for me. ....

5. Hang up your coat in the wardrobe. ....

6. Monica is not a very tall girl. ....

For Questions 7–10, write S *if the sentence is a statement or* C *if it is a command.*

*(**Hint**: If the sentence is a command, it is telling you to do something.)*

7. Feed the cat before you go and play. ....

8. Mix water into the paints. ....

9. The ice-cream melted in the hot sun. ....

10. Our house is across the street from the school. ....

My score: $\frac{}{10}$

My time: ....
  minutes   seconds

Minute 10

Name: .... **Date:** ....

Write the correct end punctuation mark for each sentence.

(Hint: Use a fullstop (.) *at the end of a statement or a command; a question* mark (?) *at the end of a question; and an exclamation mark (!) at the end of an exclamation.)*

1. What kind of cereal do you like ....

2. Shopping with my mum is fun ....

3. Tell Justin to come inside the house ....

4. Donna bought a pair of shoes for her new dress ....

5. I just won a brand-new bike ....

6. Can Pam go to the cinema with us ....

7. Put on your coat before you go outside ....

8. Wow, I just swam 12 laps in a row ....

9. Why did the little puppy run away ....

10. I like to watch scary films ....

My score:

$$\frac{}{10}$$

My time: ....
                         minutes   seconds

Complete sentences – review

Name: .... **Date:** ....

For Questions 1–6, write C if the sentence is complete or I if it is incomplete.

1. Got dressed quickly. ....

2. Gary climbed to the top of the tree. ....

3. Barry rakes the leaves in the garden. ....

4. Nicole turned off all of the lights. ....

5. Makes a delicious cheesecake. ....

6. The crackers in the kitchen. ....

For Questions 7–10, circle the sentence that is complete in each pair.

7. (a) The dog chases his tail in a circle.
   (b) The big dog on the grass.

8. (a) Louise and her sister, Nancy.
   (b) The sisters do everything together.

9. (a) Always helping my mother.
   (b) I am helping my mother today.

10. (a) The man walks on the beach.
    (b) Walks along the beach.

My score:

$\dfrac{}{10}$

My time: ....
minutes   seconds

Minute 12

Name: .... **Date:** ....

For Questions 1–7, circle the sentence in each pair that is in the correct word order.

1. (a) My grandfather has pigs, cows and horses on his farm.
   (b) Pigs, cows and horses on his farm my has grandfather.

2. (a) My write favourite thing to do is poetry.
   (b) My favourite thing to do is write poetry.

3. (a) I ate cheese and crackers when I got home.
   (b) Cheese and crackers home when I got I ate.

4. (a) Molly made bran muffins for breakfast.
   (b) Breakfast for made Molly bran muffins.

5. (a) Plays the drums oldest brother my.
   (b) My oldest brother plays the drums.

6. (a) Moved to my grandparents the country.
   (b) My grandparents moved to the country.

7. (a) We are eating at a restaurant tonight.
   (b) At restaurant eating a we are tonight.

For Questions 8–10, write each sentence in the correct word order.

8. Thomas team leader is a good.

   ....

9. The market at milk I got.

   ....

10. His arm playing football Jim broke.

   ....

My score: $\dfrac{}{10}$

My time: ....
minutes   seconds

Name: .... **Date:** ....

Read each sentence and write **S** *if the subject is underlined or* **P** *if the predicate is underlined.*

1. <u>The little girl</u> wants a pony for her birthday.   ....

2. His family <u>moved here from Ipswich.</u>   ....

3. The roof on the house <u>is too old.</u>   ....

4. <u>All of our balloons</u> blew away.   ....

5. <u>My mum</u> likes drinking orange juice.   ....

6. <u>We</u> went for a ride in a hot air balloon.   ....

7. The painters <u>got covered with paint.</u>   ....

8. Marcia and Charles <u>are cousins.</u>   ....

9. <u>They</u> watch television every night.   ....

10. <u>The lost baby</u> cried for his mummy.   ....

My score: $\dfrac{}{10}$ **My time:** ....
                                                  minutes   seconds

Minute 14

Name: .... **Date:** ....

Read each sentence and write the type of sentence it is on the line. Put S for statement, Q for question, E for exclamation or C for command.

1. Cut the paper in half. ....

2. Will you help me with my homework? ....

3. That squirrel almost bit me! ....

4. Please make up your bed. ....

5. I am going shopping for shoes. ....

6. How do you put the paint on the wall? ....

7. I swam all day in the pool. ....

8. Mix together the eggs and sugar. ....

9. The biscuits in the oven are done. ....

10. I had so much fun at Fred's house! ....

My score: $\dfrac{}{10}$

My time: ....
minutes   seconds

Minute 15

Name: .... **Date:** ....

Write the correct end punctuation mark for each sentence.

(**Hint**: Use a fullstop (.) at the end of a statement or a command; a question mark (?) at the end of a question; and an exclamation mark (!) at the end of an exclamation.)

1. The butterflies all flew out at once ....

2. Did you break my pen ....

3. Wow, the dolphins jumped out of the water ....

4. Why are Darryl and Sal going to Canada ....

5. Take out your scissors, crayons and glue ....

6. That was a terrific magic show ....

7. The doctor gave me medicine to take ....

8. The baby cried when the milk was all gone ....

9. I just won a brand-new computer ....

10. What should I get her for her birthday ....

My score:
$$\frac{\quad}{10}$$

My time: ....
minutes   seconds

Minute 16

Name: .... **Date:** ....

Circle the 10 nouns in the box. Write each noun in the chart where it belongs.

school	firefighter	computer	playground
yawned	basketball	walked	kind
beautiful	teacher	Matt	quickly
notebook	Sydney Opera House	pillow	sleepy

Person	Place	Thing
1.	4.	7. ....
2.	5.	8. ....
3.	6.	9. ....
		10. ....

My score: $\dfrac{}{10}$

My time: ....
minutes   seconds

www.prim-ed.com   Prim-Ed Publishing®

Minute 17

Name: .... **Date:** ....

Circle the two nouns in each sentence.

1. Mary went into the city all alone.

2. Ms Chow baked fresh bread.

3. Go and buy a big blanket for our picnic.

4. Her skin got burned in the sun.

5. Dr Seuss is a famous author.

6. The twins wore old-fashioned costumes.

7. The boys washed our cars for free.

8. Doris can't find her glasses.

9. The bookstore has interesting magazines.

10. The horses walk across the field.

My score: $\dfrac{}{10}$ **My time:** ....
minutes   seconds

Minute 18

Name: .... **Date:** ....

For Questions 1–6, write Yes if the underlined word is a common noun or No if it is not.

(**Hint:** A common noun *names any person, place or thing.*)

1. <u>Betsy</u> ate pizza for lunch.   ....

2. Carol is my little <u>sister</u>.   ....

3. Jody likes to shop at <u>Balmain Centre</u>.   ....

4. I can't wait to learn how to drive a <u>car</u>!   ....

5. We baked a <u>ham</u> and a turkey.   ....

6. Dawn gave her dog, <u>Oscar</u>, a bath.   ....

For Questions 7–10, circle the two common nouns in each set of words.

7. China   country   city   Athens

8. Laura   Mrs Kim   girl   woman

9. bunny   Bambi   deer   Bugs

10. street   First Street   Main Lane   lane

My score: ___
10

My time: ....
                     minutes   seconds

Minute 19

Name: .... **Date:** ....

Circle the 10 proper nouns in the box.

(**Hint**: A proper noun *names a specific person, place or thing.*)

Dr Thomas	mountain	apron
rainbow	Waterford	India
kitchen	wallet	book
Saturday	doctor	Mothering Sunday
Mt Everest	Halloween	water
country	December	Ocean Land
Prince Harry	library	water

My score: $\dfrac{}{10}$ **My time:** ....
                                        minutes   seconds

Minute 20

Name: ....   Date: ....

Circle the proper nouns in the sentences, then write them correctly on the lines.

1. jerry made a plum pudding for christmas dinner.

   ....

2. Watching the sun set over stone mountain was exciting.

   ....

3. marcia always wakes up late on monday mornings.

   ....

4. We took our dog peaches to see dr sam.

   ....

5. My favourite story is 'hansel and gretel'.

   ....

6. We ate dinner at rick's steakhouse.

   ....

7. We are reading *stuart little* by eb white in class.

   ....

8. janice and her family took a trip to snowdonia national park.

   ....

9. july is one of the coldest months in australia.

   ....

10. They went on a trip to the grand canyon.

   ....

My score: $\dfrac{}{10}$ **My time:** ....
minutes   seconds

Minute 21

Name: .... **Date:** ....

Write each noun from the box in its correct category below.

lemonade	Saturn	Harry Potter	Australia
Dr Smith	microwave	pineapple	guitar
Aunt Becky	Boggs Primary		

Person	**Place**	**Thing**
1.	4.	7. ....
2.	5.	8. ....
3.	6.	9. ....
		10. ....

My score:

$\dfrac{}{10}$

My time: ....

minutes   seconds

Minute 22

Name: .... Date: ....

Read the letter. Circle the common nouns and proper nouns. Write them in their correct category below.

Dear Aunt Gloria

I want to tell you thank you for the doll you sent me for my birthday in May. Now I have one from every country in Asia. She is so beautiful. I have decided to name her Ming. I am going to put her in my room. Thank you again for the beautiful present.

Love always

Elaine

Common	Proper
1.	6. ....
2.	7. ....
3.	8. ....
4.	9. ....
5.	10. ....

My score: $\dfrac{}{10}$

My time: ....

minutes   seconds

Minute 23

Name: .... Date: ....

For Questions 1–5, circle the correct subject pronoun to replace the underlined word or words in each sentence.

(Hint: A subject pronoun *takes the place of one or more nouns in the subject of a sentence.)*

1. <u>Ryan and Bryan</u> are twins.

   They   Them

2. <u>The dog</u> ate his food quickly.

   Him   He

3. <u>Bobby and I</u> love to go surfing at the beach.

   We   Us

4. <u>Karen</u> rakes leaves with her big brother.

   Her   She

5. <u>The microphone</u> was turned off.

   It   He

For Questions 6–10, write a pronoun to replace the underlined word or words in each sentence.

6. <u>Jonathan</u> writes a letter to his teacher. ....

7. <u>My mother</u> makes the best peach crumble. ....

8. <u>The bears</u> catch the fish from the river. ....

9. <u>Brenda and I</u> ate lunch at The Ivy Café. ....

10. <u>The bike</u> was a great present for Tim. ....

My score: ___/10   **My time:** .... minutes   .... seconds

Minute 24

Name: .... Date: ....

For Questions 1–7, write the correct object pronoun that completes each sentence.

(Hint: An object pronoun takes the place of one or more nouns in the action part of a sentence.)

1. Brian's dad took .... to the Lions game.
   we   us

2. The teacher gave .... a sticker for being good.
   I   me

3. The costumes are for .... to wear at Halloween.
   them   they

4. Jack's mum told .... to go to his room.
   him   he

5. Tanya asked me to get a napkin for...
   it   her

6. The two girls were upset that Mary didn't invite...
   they   them

7. Mr Lee gives ....pocket money for cleaning his garden.
   us   we

For Questions 8–10, write a pronoun to replace the underlined word or words in each sentence.

8. The house at the lake was built by <u>Kurt</u>.   ....

9. <u>The car</u> needs to be washed very soon.   ....

10. My parents took <u>my sister and me</u> to the fair.   ....

My score: ___
10

My time: ....
                    minutes   seconds

www.prim-ed.com   Prim-Ed Publishing®

Minute 25

Name: .... Date: ....

Write the correct possessive pronoun to complete each sentence.

(Hint: A possessive pronoun is a pronoun that shows ownership. It takes the place of one or more nouns. Possessive pronouns include my, your, his, her, our, its and their.)

1. That bike belongs to me. It is .... bike.

her   my

2. Carrie spilled juice all over .... new dress.

its   her

3. Mum got that book for John. It is .... book.

his   our

4. That old plane is missing .... left wing.

their   its

5. Our dog licked Frank's face. .... face was all wet.

His   Your

6. You are a mess! .... shirt is covered in mud.

Your   His

7. Mike and Maria are visiting .... friends today.

its   their

8. The sick dog hurt .... back leg.

our   its

9. Dad said .... family's new car is black.

his   our

10. Grandma sent .... birthday gift to me in the post.

my   its

My score: $\frac{}{10}$

My time: ....

minutes   seconds

Minute 26

Name: .... **Date:** ....

Circle the possessive pronoun in each sentence.

1. Jeff is excited about his birthday party.

2. Did your invitation come in the post yet?

3. I got my new dress yesterday.

4. Alexis is driving in her new car.

5. The kids gave their old toys away.

6. Jessica saw her favourite film again.

7. Have you seen my science book?

8. The lion dropped its prey and ran away.

9. Why can't we bring our puppy into bed?

10. Julio saw his teacher at the supermarket.

My score: ___

10

My time: ....
minutes   seconds

Minute 27

Name: .... **Date:** ....

Write each noun from the box in its correct category below.

| hospital | Dr Watson | nurse | book | librarian |
| medicine | blanket | library | table | office |

Person	Place	Thing
1.	4.	7. ....
2.	5.	8. ....
3.	6.	9. ....
		10. ....

My score: $\dfrac{}{10}$

My time: ....
minutes   seconds

Minute 28

Name: .... **Date:** ....

Circle the common noun and underline the proper noun in each sentence.

1. Frank wants to learn how to fly planes.

2. Barbara knows how to knit jumpers.

3. The bunny chased Cindy around and around.

4. Judy exercises at the park.

5. My older sister is going to Oxford University.

6. There are a lot of boats on Lake Grace.

7. Our class is studying William Shakespeare.

8. That man is from Norway.

9. My birthday is not until November.

10. Eve finally moved back home.

My score: —— / 10

My time: .... minutes .... seconds

www.prim-ed.com Prim-Ed Publishing®

Minute 29

Name: .... **Date:** ....

For Questions 1–5, circle the correct pronoun to replace the underlined word or words in each sentence.

1. <u>Amy and Nick</u> are going to the concert.
   They   Them

2. I made breakfast for <u>my parents</u> this morning.
   them   us

3. <u>Jacob</u> wants a new bike for his birthday.
   He   Him

4. <u>My sister and I</u> take tennis lessons.
   Us   We

5. My mum said to call <u>Sheila</u> on the phone.
   she   her

For Questions 6–10, write a pronoun to replace the underlined word or words in each sentence.

6. <u>Claudia and I</u> were surprised to see Lou. ....

7. <u>Sharon</u> bought a bracelet for her mother. ....

8. Allison is taking <u>Stephanie and me</u> to the park. ....

9. Please give the salt to <u>Henry</u>. ....

10. <u>Anthony and his brother</u> have bunk beds. ....

My score: $\dfrac{\quad}{10}$ **My time:** ....
                                                minutes   seconds

Minute 30

Name: .... Date: ....

For Questions 1–6, circle the possessive pronoun in each sentence.

1. Dorothy cut her own hair at home.

2. Has anyone seen my pink slippers?

3. The rugs in our house are being cleaned.

4. Doug said that his computer is broken.

5. Eileen's parents had their wedding in Greece.

6. The poor cow was pushed on its side.

For Questions 7–10, read the pair of sentences. Write a possessive pronoun on the line to complete the second sentence.

(**Hint**: The possessive pronoun *replaces a noun in the first sentence.*)

7. Is this Adam's phone? Yes, it is .... phone.

8. Do you have Vicky's bag? No, I don't have .... bag.

9. Does this house belong to Matt and Joey? Yes, this is .... house.

10. Have you seen the hamster's cage? No, I haven't seen .... cage.

My score: $\overline{}$
10

My time: ....
minutes   seconds

Minute 31

Name: .... **Date:** ....

Write the plural form for each noun.

(**Hint**: These plural nouns *end in -s, -es or -ies.*)

1. baby ....

2. class ....

3. rope ....

4. computer ....

5. trumpet ....

6. porch ....

7. box ....

8. lady ....

9. kitten ....

10. city ....

My score: $\frac{}{10}$

My time: .... minutes .... seconds

Minute 32

Name: .... **Date:** ....

Write the correct plural noun to complete each sentence.

1. The firefighter told us to never play with ....
    matches   matchs

2. Our librarian always reads the best .... to us.
    storys   stories

3. Please sharpen these .... for the class.
    pencils   penciles

4. The two .... have long, bushy tails.
    foxs   foxes

5. We bought five .... at the fruit stall.
    peaches   peachies

6. Four .... were sleeping in the tree.
    owls   owlies

7. We learned about nocturnal ...., such as foxes.
    animals   animales

8. Simon and Walter put ....on their vanilla cupcakes.
    cherrys   cherries

9. Many .... are entering the writing contest.
    pupiles   pupils

10. The .... were all different colours.
    butterflys   butterflies

My score: $\overline{10}$

My time: ....
                    minutes   seconds

www.prim-ed.com   Prim-Ed Publishing®

Minute 33

Name: .... Date: ....

Circle the singular noun and underline the plural noun in each sentence.

1. The dog waited for his owners to return.

2. These candles on the table smell good.

3. The bird caught two worms to eat.

4. Our umbrellas are in that bucket.

5. The two poodles belong to my neighbour.

6. The zebras were moved to the zoo.

7. Our new glasses broke in the box.

8. The strings on my guitar are brand new.

9. My friends drove by in a red car.

10. The girl collected many seashells.

My score: ——
10

My time: ....
minutes   seconds

Minute 34

Name: .... Date: ....

Write the correct noun to complete each sentence.

1. Sarah collected five .... for her album.

sticker   stickers

2. Please help me put my .... through the loops.

belt   belts

3. The ....takes good care of his animals.

farmer   farmers

4. The fans wore black and white football .... to the
   match.

scarf   scarves

5. I only have enough money to buy one new video...

game   games

6. David helped his mother wash all the...

window   windows

7. I picked a bunch of ....from our tree.

orange   oranges

8. My mum bought three pairs of ....for my dad.

sock   socks

9. One ....swam behind all the other ducks

duck   ducks
   in the pond.

10. Matt ordered one large ....for dinner.

pizza   pizzas

My score: ____
10

My time: ....

minutes   seconds

Minute 35

Name: ....

Date: ....

Write the plural form for each noun.

1. wolf ....

2. foot ....

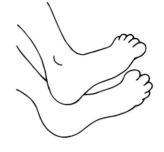

3. tooth ....

4. child ....

5. life ....

6. man ....

7. mouse ....

8. shelf ....

9. goose ....

10. sheep ....

My score: $\dfrac{}{10}$

My time: ....
            minutes   seconds

Name: .... **Date:** ....

Circle the incorrect noun in each sentence, then write it correctly on the line.

*(**Hint**: Each sentence has one* singular noun *that must be changed to a plural noun.)*

1. The leaf change from green to yellow in the autumn.   ....

2. They are all playing elf in the school play.   ....

3. There are six person shopping in the store.   ....

4. The three woman wore pretty dresses today.   ....

5. Two ox are walking slowly in the field.   ....

6. I saw two mouse run by with cheese.   ....

7. My new pair of shoes hurt my foot all day.   ....

8. The mother cow is feeding her three calf.   ....

9. All of the child went on the class excursion.   ....

10. Take out five knife for the dinner table.   ....

My score:
—
10

My time: ....
                          minutes   seconds

Minute 37

Name: .... **Date:** ....

Circle the noun in each sentence that needs to show ownership. Write its possessive form ('s) on the line.

*(**Hint**: Adding 's to a noun makes it possessive, or shows ownership; for example: Maria's bag.)*

1. Jason book report was the best in the class.   ....

2. The horse saddle was strapped to its back.   ....

3. Mona parents threw her a birthday party.   ....

4. An elephant trunk is very strong.   ....

5. Tom science project gained top marks.   ....

6. The little girl pink dress was perfect for Easter.   ....

7. Wendy dinner party was a lot of fun.   ....

8. The basketball team bus broke down after the game.   ....

9. Have you seen your sister homework?   ....

10. Yesterday trip to the museum took all day.   ....

My score: ___

10

My time: ....
minutes   seconds

Minute 38

Name: .... **Date:** ....

Rewrite each plural noun in brackets as a plural possessive noun.

*(**Hint**: A plural possessive noun shows ownership by more than one person or thing. When a plural noun ends in -s, adding an apostrophe (') to the end makes it possessive; for example: the sisters' room.)*

1. The five (girls) baskets were full of sweets. ....

2. Our (grandparents) farm has lots of horses to ride. ....

3. The (pupils) coats were neatly hung on the pegs. ....

4. My three (brothers) beds are in the same room. ....

5. We put our (friends) gifts on their desks. ....

6. The (firefighters) uniforms were dirty. ....

7. The (kids) dad got back from his trip yesterday. ....

8. My (dogs) tails wag fast when they see their food. ....

9. All the (classes) pictures were taken today. ....

10. The (birds) wings flapped quickly in the air. ....

My score:
___
10

My time: ....
minutes   seconds

Minute 39

Name: .... **Date:** ....

Circle the collective noun in each sentence.

(Hint: A collective noun names a group of people, animals or things. For example, a flock of birds means a group of birds that stay together.)

1. The army of ants marched through the kitchen.

2. My pair of socks has lots of holes.

3. A herd of cattle relaxed in the tall green grass.

4. A pack of dogs ran through our front garden.

5. I saw a great picture of a galaxy of stars.

6. Dina wanted to join the chorus at her school.

7. I do not like being in a crowd of people.

8. I ate a stack of pancakes for breakfast.

9. I have a pile of homework tonight.

10. A swarm of bees chased my dog.

My score: ──── **My time:** ....
10   minutes   seconds

Minute 40

Name: ....   Date: ....

Use a collective noun from the box to complete each sentence.

fleet	flock	cast	litter	team
stack	family	crew	bundle	deck

1. My mum gave me a .... of three pancakes.

2. Stephen's .... won the football match.

3. The .... on the ship was very nice to us when we arrived.

4. I bought a .... of cards to play Snap with my friends.

5. The .... of birds flew to the telephone pole.

6. A lot of .... members came to my sister's graduation.

7. The .... of actors for our school play all got sick.

8. A .... of ships lined the shore in our city.

9. My cat had a .... of kittens last week.

10. My dad took a .... of clothes to the charity shop.

My score:
$\dfrac{\quad}{10}$

My time: ....
                     minutes   seconds

Minute 41

Name: .... **Date:** ....

Circle the correct plural noun in each set of words.

1. buddies   buddy   buddyes

2. faceies   faces   facies

3. classies   classs   classes

4. toys   toies   toyes

5. pianos   pianoes   pianies

6. daies   days   dayies

7. prizees   prizies   prizes

8. bunnys   bunnies   bunnyes

9. foxes   foxs   foxies

10. computeres   computeries   computers

My score: $\dfrac{}{10}$

My time: .... minutes .... seconds

Name: .... **Date:** ....

Write the correct noun to complete each sentence.

1. My dog has lots of .... on his face.
   whisker   whiskers

2. Sam took five .... to the picnic.
   cake   cakes

3. The caterpillar was about five .... long.
   centimetre   centimetres

4. Linh gave her best ...., Chloe, a gift.
   friend   friends

5. The surfer rode the many high .... at the beach.
   wave   waves

6. My .... is being fixed.
   computer   computers

7. I saved one thousand .... in my piggy bank.
   coin   coins

8. Mary went shopping for a party ....
   dress   dresses

9. Our large family needed two .... for Christmas.
   turkey   turkeys

10. I don't like .... in my salad.
    tomato   tomatoes

My score:

10

My time: ....
                  minutes   seconds

www.prim-ed.com   Prim-Ed Publishing®

Minute 43

Name: .... Date: ....

Circle the correct plural form for each word in bold.

1. **calf**   calves   calfs

2. **deer**   deer   deers

3. **child**   children   childs

4. **wife**   wifes   wives

5. **potato**   potatos   potatoes

6. **tooth**   toothes   teeth

7. **torpedo**   torpedoes   torpedos

8. **loaf**   loaves   loafes

9. **sheep**   sheeps   sheep

10. **woman**   women   womans

My score: $\dfrac{}{10}$

My time: ....
                    minutes   seconds

Minute 44

Name: .... **Date:** ....

Circle the possessive noun in each sentence. Write S if it is a singular possessive noun or P if it is a plural possessive noun.

1. The cat's yarn was tangled in his paws. ....

2. The house's roof has a leak. ....

3. The pupils' favourite book is *The cat in the hat*. ....

4. Elaine's aeroplane ticket was in the bottom of her bag. ....

5. Ali's dance moves were the best in the troupe. ....

6. The classes' test scores were the highest in the school. ....

7. Lindsey's ring was bright and shiny. ....

8. The baby birds' mother went to get them food. ....

9. The cup's handle is broken and can't be used. ....

10. Trevor's car was in the garage for two days. ....

My score: ── **My time:** ....
10   minutes   seconds

Name: .... **Date:** ....

Circle the collective noun in each sentence.

1. The audience cheered when I finished my song.

2. A couple of doves are sitting on that tree.

3. A cluster of pupils gathered to see the experiment.

4. Mrs Cooper has a collection of crystal figures.

5. The colony of ants built many ant hills in my garden.

6. A mob of kangaroos travelled together to find water.

7. My portfolio of pictures won second place in the photo contest.

8. The police squad chased the bank robbers.

9. A school of fish swam together in the ocean.

10. The chess team was excited to win first place.

My score:

$$\frac{}{10}$$

My time:

....

minutes   seconds

Name: .... **Date:** ....

Circle the verb in each sentence.

(Hint: A verb is a word that shows action.)

1. The baby waved bye to his mother.

2. The bird chirped loudly in the tree.

3. Please take your medicine now.

4. Linda wanted the lead role in the play.

5. Next, we knead the dough for the bread.

6. The tyre rolled down the street.

7. Philippa rested peacefully on the sofa.

8. Shuffle the cards before the card game.

9. Finn and James ran four laps around the track.

10. Veronica sneezed all night long.

My score: $\dfrac{}{10}$

My time: ....
minutes   seconds

Minute 47

Name: .... Date: ....

Circle the 10 verbs in the box. Write them on the lines below.

sweep	squeak	read	wink	heart
invitation	scare	sprint	piano	prance
broom	raincoat	caterpillar	grow	prince
growl	ribbon	mumble	keyboard	aeroplane

1. ....

2. ....

3. ....

4. ....

5. ....

6. ....

7. ....

8. ....

9. ....

10. ....

My score:
$$\frac{}{10}$$

My time: ....
minutes   seconds

Minute 48

Name: .... **Date:** ....

Write the verb with the correct tense for each sentence.

1. Rachel just .... her pencil before it broke.
   sharpens   sharpened

2. Jamie .... Lisa with a special gift yesterday.
   surprises   surprised

3. The dog .... at the moon all night.
   howling   howled

4. She is .... a secret in Vivian's ear.
   whispering   whispered

5. We will always .... St Patrick's Day each year.
   celebrate   celebrated

6. Gino .... in his sleep last night.
   talks   talked

7. The girl .... after the boy pulled her hair.
   cries   cried

8. Dave still .... the same show every day.
   watches   watched

9. Courtney .... loudly when she wants something.
   yells   yelled

10. Penny .... this afternoon after running in the race.
    rests   rested

My score: $\overline{10}$

My time: ....
minutes   seconds

Minute 49

Name: .... Date: ....

Write the present and past tense forms of each verb on the lines.

Verb	Present tense	Past tense
1. shout	He .... loudly.	He .... loudly.
2. honk	She .... the horn.	She .... the horn.
3. blink	I .... my eyes.	I .... my eyes.
4. smile	They .... at me.	They .... at me.
5. gallop	It .... gracefully.	It .... gracefully.
6. hope	We .... for rain.	We .... for rain.
7. snore	He .... a lot.	He .... a lot.
8. sniff	The dog .... me.	The dog .... me.
9. ask	They .... questions.	They .... questions.
10. bake	She .... biscuits.	She .... biscuits.

My score:

—
10

My time: ....

minutes   seconds

Name: .... **Date:** ....

For Questions 1–5, use the verbs in the box to complete each sentence.

| am | is | are | was | were |

1. I .... the shortest girl in my class right now.

2. All of my friends .... now taller than me.

3. Lilly .... sad when her puppy ran away.

4. Larry .... the funniest person I know.

5. We .... home all last night.

For Questions 6–10, circle the correct verb to complete each sentence.

6. Christopher (are, is) a talented basketball player.

7. Elliot and Olivia (were, are) famous detectives now.

8. I (is, am) the only girl in the family.

9. The ceiling fan (was, is) dirty before I cleaned it.

10. The puppies (are, were) much smaller two weeks ago.

My score: ___ / 10

My time: ....
minutes   seconds

Minute 51

Name: .... Date: ....

Write the correct verb to complete each sentence.

1. Sandra's water .... cold and refreshing.

is   are

2. I .... two years older than you are.

am   are

3. We .... tired when we got back from the beach.

are   were

4. Ross .... Monica's older brother.

is   are

5. The kids .... outside with their friends now.

are   were

6. Last year's fireworks .... better than this year's.

are   were

7. James did not go to school because he .... sick.

was   were

8. That .... still my favourite book.

is   are

9. I .... the team's captain all next week.

am   was

10. They .... both last year's best pupils.

was   were

My score: $\dfrac{}{10}$

My time: ....

minutes   seconds

Minute 52

Name: ....   **Date:** ....

Using the information in the box, circle the helping verb in each sentence.

	Helping verb	*Main verb*	
He	is	talking	to me.
We	were	jogging	yesterday.
I	have	finished	my work.
She	has	called	two times.

1. I have learned a lot of words in French.

2. Victoria is eating dinner at our house tonight.

3. We are buying her a nice gift for Mothering Sunday.

4. My teacher has visited me at my house before.

5. I was reading in bed when the storm started.

6. The pupils were working quietly at their desks.

7. David has dropped the chocolate cake on the floor.

8. I am writing a thank-you letter to my grandma.

9. The birds have eaten all the seeds on the bird table.

10. The girls were jumping rope at break.

My score: $\overline{}$

10

My time: ....

                                      minutes   seconds

Name: .... **Date:** ....

Write Yes *if the underlined helping verb is used correctly or* No *if it is not.*

1. We <u>is</u> travelling to Edinburgh to visit my aunt. ....

2. Rene and Julie <u>are</u> saving their money. ....

3. Thao <u>has</u> painted a picture for his parents. ....

4. Mrs Gomez <u>have</u> stopped teaching already. ....

5. They <u>are</u> studying for their maths quiz. ....

6. Ruth <u>has</u> scored in the last two hockey games. ....

7. My mum <u>has</u> planning a surprise party for my brother. ....

8. Our neighbours <u>have</u> borrowed our lawnmower. ....

9. I <u>am</u> climbing the tree to rescue the kitten. ....

1 0. My dad <u>has</u> walked on the Great Wall of China. ....

My score: $\dfrac{}{10}$

My time: ....
minutes   seconds

Minute 54

Name: .... **Date:** ....

Using the information in the box, circle the verb that best completes each sentence.

(**Hint**: Irregular verbs *do not end in -ed in the past tense.*)

Present	Past	Past with helping verb
eat, eats	ate	(have, has, had) eaten
give, gives	gave	(have, has, had) given
buy, buys	bought	(have, has, had) bought

1. Joanna (sweeped, swept) the kitchen floor after dinner.

2. My Uncle Cliff (bit, bited) into an apple and chipped his tooth.

3. Alicia (took, take) many pairs of jeans on her holiday.

4. My dad has (builded, built) many things in our house.

5. We (feeded, fed) our dog before we left for the day.

6. They have (driven, drive) the same car for twenty years!

7. Janet had (forgets, forgotten) to set the alarm clock.

8. The roses (froze, freezed) outside during the winter months.

9. Claire (weared, wore) a dress last night to the dance.

10. Julio (hang, hung) his jacket up in his wardrobe.

My score:

$\dfrac{}{10}$

My time: ....
                                        minutes   seconds

Minute 55

Name: .... **Date:** ....

For each sentence, write the correct past-tense form for the verb under the line.

1. The wind .... the leaves off the trees.
   blow

2. Phil .... me for his kickball team.
   choose

3. Marcia .... from Perth to Sydney.
   drive

4. I was so thirsty, I .... five glasses of water.
   drink

5. We have .... at that restaurant before.
   eat

6. The plane .... right over our house.
   fly

7. I .... my homework twice last week.
   forget

8. My aunt has .... us a lot of nice books.
   give

9. The phone .... once before I answered.
   ring

10. Sylvia has .... lots of poems and stories.
    write

My score: ────
10

My time: ....
minutes   seconds

Minute 56

Name: .... **Date:** ....

Circle the verb in each sentence.

1. William grills hamburgers on the barbecue.

2. Lauren clapped loudly during the show.

3. Walter and Heidi hike mountains together.

4. I play golf with my dad every Saturday.

5. The children followed the teacher to the office.

6. Amanda's mum teaches Japanese classes.

7. The caterpillar changed into a beautiful butterfly.

8. Kyle's family enjoyed their picnic at the beach.

9. The cat rips the sofa with its sharp nails.

10. The girls giggled at the clown's tricks.

My score: ___
10

My time: ....
minutes   seconds

www.prim-ed.com   Prim-Ed Publishing®

Name: .... **Date:** ....

Write the verb with the correct tense in each sentence.

1. I .... up so high, I hurt my arm.
   reach   reached

2. My mouse .... my sister when he escaped.
   scares   scared

3. My mum .... us muffins whenever we ask nicely.
   bakes   baked

4. Our dog .... when the cat ran by the window.
   barks   barked

5. My dad ....loudly right now because he has a cold.
   snores   snored

6. The baby .... every time I tickle her tummy.
   smiles   smiled

7. The ball .... twice in the air before I caught it.
   bounce   bounced

8. The tiger .... as the zookeeper enters the cage.
   growls   growled

9. Justin .... the table so hard, he broke his toe.
   kick   kicked

10. We .... a scary film late last night.
    watch   watched

My score: $\dfrac{}{10}$ **My time:** ....
                                                              minutes   seconds

Minute 58

Name: .... **Date:** ....

Circle the linking verb in each sentence.

1. Brad and Chad are cousins.

2. I am a better pupil this year than last year.

3. Mr Smith was not my teacher last year.

4. My Aunt Noeline was sick last week.

5. Samantha and Jackie were friends in nursery.

6. Joey is the fastest runner in the school.

7. Carol was shorter than Kathy last year.

8. The girls were cold out in the rain.

9. I am the teacher's helper this month.

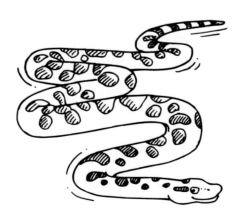

10. That snake is Graham's newest pet.

My score: $\dfrac{}{10}$ **My time:** ....
minutes   seconds

Minute 59

Name: .... **Date:** ....

Using the information in the box, circle the helping verb and underline the main verb in each sentence.

	Helping verb	**Main verb**	
He	is	talking	to me.
We	were	jogging	yesterday.
I	have	finished	my work.
She	has	called	two times.

1. We have sent everyone an invitation.

2. Mary has skateboarded around the playground five times.

3. Pam is walking to the park with her sister.

4. I am putting the groceries away for my mother.

5. All the classes have taken pictures for the yearbook.

6. Jessica has been a ballet dancer for two years.

7. My uncle is building a tree house for us.

8. The kids are listening to music.

9. Alan has lived in France and Spain.

10. My mum is waiting for us outside.

My score: ——
10

My time: ....
                     minutes   seconds

Minute 60

Name: .... Date: ....

Write the correct past-tense verb form to complete each sentence.

1. We .... our homework at the kitchen table.
   did   done

2. She .... up all night worrying about her sick cat.
   was   been

3. My mum has .... me for lying to her.
   forgave   forgiven

4. I have .... to never lie to my mum again.
   swore   sworn

5. Denise .... a horse on the farm last summer.
   rode   ridden

6. The poor bird had .... right into the window.
   flew   flown

7. She accidentally .... the ball over the fence.
   threw   thrown

8. Our class has never .... in trouble before.
   was   been

9. We .... lots of vegetables in our old garden.
   grew   grown

10. My parents have .... to my teacher about my marks.
    spoke   spoken

My score: ____
10

My time: ....
         minutes   seconds

Name: .... **Date:** ....

Circle the adjective in each sentence.

*(**Hint**: An adjective is a word that describes a noun.)*

1. Marcus won a blue ribbon in the contest.

2. I like to paint on a smooth surface.

3. The flowers he gave me are pink.

4. There are five apples in the bowl.

5. The strong man picked up all the boxes.

6. The perfume had a fruity scent.

7. The sick puppy slept all day.

8. Your idea for the project is great!

9. It was a gloomy day.

10. I am going to adopt the white bunny.

My score: $\frac{}{10}$

My time: ....
minutes   seconds

Minute 62

Name: .... Date: ....

Write the correct adjective in each sentence.

(**Hint**: *Adjectives that end in -er compare two things, and adjectives that end in -est compare more than two things.*)

1. Our new stereo system sounds much .... than our old one.
    louder   loudest

2. This ice-cream shop has the .... lemon sorbet.
    better   best

3. That is the .... hamster I have ever seen.
    smaller   smallest

4. I think *Shrek* is .... than *Shrek 2*.
    funnier   funniest

5. My dad is two years .... than my mum.
    younger   youngest

6. Floyd is the .... cat of all.
    noisier   noisiest

7. Wendy is always the .... to arrive.
    later   latest

8. I got to school .... than her today.
    earlier   earliest

9. My grandfather is the .... man I know.
    wiser   wisest

10. This book is .... than the last book I read.
    longer   longest

My score: ___/10

My time: ....
         minutes   seconds

Minute 63

Name: .... **Date:** ....

Circle the adverb in each sentence. Write how, when, or where **to tell what the adverb describes.**

*(**Hint**: An adverb is a word that describes a verb and tells how, when or where something happens.)*

1. Sean happily cleaned his room. ....

2. Geraldine raised her hand shyly to ask a question. ....

3. I ran downstairs to answer the front door. ....

4. Steve is going surfing tomorrow. ....

5. The runner quickly finished the race. ....

6. Jasmine had to put her dog outside. ....

7. The lion meanly glared at us through the glass. ....

8. The artist paints daily in his art studio. ....

9. My father proudly told everyone I made
   the honour roll. ....

10. I take my younger sister everywhere I go. ....

My score:

$\dfrac{}{10}$

My time: ....
                     minutes   seconds

Minute 64

Name: .... **Date:** ....

For Questions 1–5, use the adverbs in the box to complete each sentence.

| near | often | proudly | inside | sadly |

1. The teacher came running .... the room.

2. Sydney's mum .... told her that her hamster died.

3. We .... go to the same place to eat lunch.

4. The ice-cream shop is .... my house.

5. Calvin .... showed everyone his award.

For Questions 6–10, use the adverbs in the box to complete each sentence.

| carefully | under | loudly | far | Sometimes |

6. The supermarket is .... away from our house.

7. She .... held her grandmother's glass vase.

8. The scared cat ran .... the bed to hide.

9. .... we see my teacher at the library.

10. She .... screamed when the car almost hit us.

My score:

$\dfrac{}{10}$

My time: ....
            minutes   seconds

www.prim-ed.com Prim-Ed Publishing®

Minute 65

Name: .... Date: ....

For Questions 1–5, draw a line to match each beginning of a compound word with its ending. Write the complete compound word on the line.

1. pop   shelf   ....

2. book   light   ....

3. home   corn   ....

4. sun   bird   ....

5. black   work   ....

For Questions 6–10, write a compound word using two words from each description.

6. a book for my notes   ....

7. a lace for my shoe   ....

8. a board used to skate with   ....

9. the flakes from which snow is made   ....

10. an ache in the head   ....

My score: $\frac{}{10}$

My time: ....
                minutes   seconds

Minute 66

Name: .... Date: ....

For Questions 1–5, use the words in the box to write five different compound words.

star	heart	toe	sweet	table
sun	cloth	fish	set	nail

1. ....

2. ....

3. ....

4. ....

5. ....

For Questions 6–10, use the words in the box to write five different compound words.

craft	flower	rain	sun	bow
cake	way	pan	space	drive

6. ....

7. ....

8. ....

9. ....

10. ....

My score: $\dfrac{}{10}$

My time: ....
minutes   seconds

www.prim-ed.com   Prim-Ed Publishing®

Name: .... **Date:** ....

Write Yes if the commas are in the correct place or No if they are not.

1. We need apples oranges, and pears. ....

2. Rio de, Janeiro Brazil ....

3. In 2011, nine teams played basketball nationally. ....

4. London, England ....

5. Donegal Ireland, ...

6. He, has holidays in December January and February. ....

7. New York, USA ....

8. You should invite Jude, Kelly and Amber. ....

9. 16 Love Lane, Lambeth, London ....

10. In 2012 18, teams will compete in the tournament. ....

My score: ___
10

My time: ....
minutes   seconds

Name: .... **Date:** ....

Insert the missing commas in each sentence.

1. Mark Veronica and Debbie are excited about their holiday.

2. Maths history and art are my favourite subjects at school.

3. We had to write if the weather was sunny cloudy or rainy.

4. I had mushrooms bacon toast and eggs for breakfast.

5. It rained last week on Sunday Monday and Tuesday.

6. We are going to visit the cities of Bristol Bath and Oxford.

7. I bought a hat scarf and gloves to match my blue winter coat.

8. Jackie's favourite books are *Animalia The giving tree* and *Bear & Chook by the sea*.

9. Luoia likes to read books about nature history and science.

10. Dina wrote about the characters setting and plot in her book report.

My score: $\dfrac{}{10}$

My time: ....
minutes   seconds

Minute 69

Name: .... **Date:** ....

Write the two words that make up each contraction.

1. can't   ....

2. I'm   ....

3. I've   ....

4. aren't   ....

5. you'll   ....

6. it's   ....

7. she's   ....

8. won't   ....

9. you're   ....

10. doesn't   ....

My score: $\dfrac{}{10}$ **My time:** ....
minutes   seconds

Minute 70

Name: .... **Date:** ....

Write the contraction for each group of words.

1. they are ....

2. he is ....

3. do not ....

4. we have ....

5. was not ....

6. you had ....

7. what is ....

8. is not ....

9. should not ....

10. she will ....

My score: $\overline{10}$ **My time:** ....
minutes   seconds

Minute 71

Name: .... **Date:** ....

Circle the adjective in each sentence.

1. Maxine is the fastest runner on the team.

2. Alisa has lavender flowers in her garden.

3. The yellow butterfly was flying in the sky.

4. That dress is nicer on you than on me.

5. The watermelon was juicy.

6. We saw a dirty car on the street.

7. The cold air froze the water.

8. The brisk wind blew over our pool.

9. His jokes were funnier this time.

10. Her ring is the brightest one.

My score:

$\dfrac{}{10}$

My time:

....
minutes   seconds

Minute 72

Name: .... **Date:** ....

Write the correct adverb to complete each sentence.

1. The boy sang .... the theatre.

inside   loudly

2. The turtle .... walked across the grass.

slowly   very

3. We missed the show because we were 10 minutes................................... .

early   late

4. Emma .... accepted her award.

happily   sadly

5. We ran .... to catch the bus.

outside   inside

6. We will go shopping for new clothes ....

today   yesterday

7. Simon ran so .... that he beat everyone.

quickly   slowly

8. The bees .... made honey in their hive.

busily   cutely

9. The apple fell .... from the tree.

down   up

10. I brush my teeth...................................

daily   weekly

My score:
$$\frac{}{10}$$

My time: ....

minutes   seconds

www.prim-ed.com   Prim-Ed Publishing®

Minute 73

Name: .... Date: ....

Circle the word that makes a compound word with the word in bold. Write the complete compound word on the line.

1. **foot** lane   path   ....

2. **barn** hay   yard   ....

3. **foot** skin   ball   ....

4. **butter** fly   moth   ....

5. **sail** boat   water   ....

6. **sun** rise   bow   ....

7. **table** cloth   plate   ....

8. **rain** wind   bow   ....

9. **text** book   page   ....

10. **door** knob   sung   ....

My score: $\frac{}{10}$

My time: ....
          minutes   seconds

Minute 74

Name: .... **Date:** ....

Insert the missing commas in the sentences.

1. I took my tent sleeping bag and fishing rod on the camping trip.

2. By 2010 23 awards had been won.

3. Ben Sarah and Nick are all cousins.

4. Mimi's family is going to Christchurch New Zealand, for a month.

5. I like that film *The goonies*, much more than the new one.

6. Nancy's favourite colours are purple pink, blue and red.

7. We rode on the roller-coaster Ferris wheel and the bumper cars at the Easter show.

8. This past summer, my teacher read books wrote poems and travelled.

9. Lisa ate grilled chicken potatoes and spinach for dinner.

10. Justine moved to Dublin from Edinburgh Scotland.

My score: ———
10

My time: ....
minutes   seconds

Minute 75

Name: .... **Date:** ....

For Questions 1–5, write the contraction for each group of words.

1. I have   ....

2. did not   ....

3. we will   ....

4. are not   ....

5. he is   ....

For Questions 6–10, circle the contraction in each sentence. Write the two words that make up each contraction on the lines.

6. You shouldn't chew gum at school.   ....

7. Did the doctor say you're better?   ....

8. I'll bring you a gift from my trip.   ....

9. We can't go to the beach after all.   ....

10. Gary hasn't been to school in two days.   ....

My score: $\dfrac{}{10}$

My time: ....
                   minutes   seconds

Name: .... Date: ....

Write each prefix from the box in front of the best word ending below. The definitions of what the complete words should mean are provided to help you.

(**Hint**: A prefix *changes the meaning of a word by adding a group of letters to the beginning of the word.*)

dis-	tri-	uni-	bi-	un-
re-	im-	non-	pre-	in-

1. .... correct (not correct)

2. .... possible (not possible)

3. .... wind (to wind back)

4. .... plan (to plan before)

5. .... angle (with three angles)

6. .... able (not able)

7. .... form (one form)

8. .... stop (not stopping)

9. .... agree (not agree)

10. .... plane (a plane with two sets of wings)

My score:
—————
10

My time: ....
minutes   seconds

Minute 77

Name: .... Date: ....

Circle the word in each sentence that ends with a suffix.

*(**Hint**: A suffix changes the meaning of a word by adding a group of letters to the end of the word.)*

1. The painter did a good job on our house.

2. I cut my left foot on the broken glass.

3. We are hopeful that our cat will get better.

4. The little girl happily skips on the grass.

5. Tanya and Carmen's friendship is special.

6. The dull scissors were useless.

7. What is the quickest way to get there?

8. Danielle shows a lot of kindness to her baby sister.

9. Robert is selfish when he doesn't think of others.

10. We were not comfortable on the hot bus.

My score: ___
10

My time: ....
minutes   seconds

Minute 78

Name: .... Date: ....

Write Yes if the sets of words are synonyms or No if they are not.

(**Hint**: A synonym is a word that means the same thing or almost the same thing.)

1. rear   behind   ....

2. shout   yell   ....

3. huge   tiny   ....

4. sorry   regretful   ....

5. smooth   bumpy   ....

6. present   gift   ....

7. capture   release   ....

8. messy   neat   ....

9. rock   stone   ....

10. brief   long   ....

My score: ___
         10

My time: ....
              minutes   seconds

Minute 79

Name: .... **Date:** ....

Write each word from the box next to its best antonym below.

(Hint: An antonym is a word that means the opposite of something.)

arrive	ugly	positive	rude	disappear
straight	shallow	blame	major	noisy

1. bent ....

2. appear ....

3. negative ....

4. forgive ....

5. depart ....

6. beautiful ....

7. quiet ....

8. polite ....

9. minor ....

10. deep ....

My score: $\frac{}{10}$

My time: ....
minutes   seconds

Minute 80

Name: .... **Date:** ....

Write the correct homophone to complete each sentence.

*(**Hint**: Homophones are words that sound the same but have different meanings and can be spelt differently.)*

1. The black .... let out a loud roar.
   bear   bare

2. The .... bird made a nest in the barn.
   blue   blew

3. My mum put a .... of cake in my lunch box.
   peace   piece

4. We can .... a story about our favourite animals.
   right   write

5. The bookcase is made from a very expensive ....
   would   wood

6. The morning .... sparkled on the grass.
   do   dew

7. Janet's .... sundress was pink with flowers.
   new   knew

8. Can you .... this button on my shirt?
   so   sew

9. The teacher asked me to read my story ....
   aloud   allowed

10. The .... outside was sunny and breezy.
    weather   whether

My score: _____
10

My time: ....
minutes   seconds

Name: .... **Date:** ....

For Questions 1–6, circle the correct meaning for the underlined homograph in each sentence.

(Hint: Homographs are words that are spelt the same—and sometimes sound the same—but have different meanings.)

1. Everyone <u>bow</u> when the curtain rises.
   a. to bend down from the waist   **b.** a knotted ribbon

2. My mum <u>plants</u> fresh flowers every spring.
   a. puts something in the ground   **b.** living things with leaves

3. The fierce <u>wind</u> blew the roof off the house.
   a. to turn   **b.** a strong current of air

4. The mayor will <u>present</u> me with my award.
   a. a gift   **b.** to give

5. One huge <u>tear</u> ran down the little girl's cheek.
   a. liquid from the eye   **b.** to rip

6. The car shop is <u>close</u> to the motorway exit.
   a. to shut   **b.** near

For Questions 7–10, match the underlined homograph in each sentence with its correct meaning.

7. We take two <u>breaks</u> during the day.   • jumped

8. He always <u>breaks</u> something when he visits.   • a small pigeon

9. The magician made a <u>dove</u> appear.   • rests

10. Mark <u>dove</u> into the water.   • damages

My score: $\frac{\quad}{10}$ **My time:** ....
minutes   seconds

Minute 82

Name: .... **Date:** ....

Write the article (a, an or the) *that best completes each sentence.*

*(**Hint**: Use **a** before words that begin with a consonant sound, and use **an** before words that begin with a vowel sound. You can use **the** before a word that begins with a consonant sound or a vowel sound. Use **the** before a word that stands for a specific person, place or thing.)*

1. We saw .... same elephant last time we came to the zoo.

2. .... book for our report is *Ramona the Brave*.

3. I asked my mother for .... cheese sandwich for lunch.

4. Drew and Nick are .... nicest boys in my class.

5. .... emu is an animal with good eyesight.

6. We might give the teacher .... gift when school ends.

7. The kids sold cookies to earn money to go to .... circus.

8. Peter ate .... orange and a banana during lunch.

9. .... children were excited that it was the last day of school.

10. They bought .... skipping-rope and a new ball at the shop.

My score: $\dfrac{\quad\quad}{10}$ **My time:** ....
                                                       minutes   seconds

Name: .... **Date:** ....

Use the prepositions in the box to best complete each sentence.

for	upon	by	between	outside
over	until	with	off	during

1. We gave Dad a watch .... Father's Day.

2. The lights were .... when we got home.

3. Melanie got sick .... school and had to go home.

4. Jennifer was going to read .... she fell asleep.

5. We will ask Grandad if he wants to go .... us.

6. I can't decide .... wearing red shoes or black shoes.

7. I placed your tennis racket .... the front door.

8. Put your coat .... there by the cupboard.

9. The frogs .... my window croaked all night.

10. Once .... a time, the handsome prince was a frog.

My score: $\dfrac{}{10}$ **My time:** ....
                                              minutes   seconds

Minute 84

Name: .... **Date:** ....

Circle the prefix or suffix in each word. Write **P** if the word begins with a prefix or **S** if it ends with a suffix.

1. disappear ....

2. bicycle ....

3. joyless ....

4. unhappy ....

5. darkness ....

6. farmer ....

7. prepay ....

8. smartest ....

9. fatherly ....

10. relive ....

My score: ——
10

My time: ....
minutes   seconds

Name: .... Date: ....

Write the missing synonym or antonym for each word in bold.

Verb	Synonym	Antonym
1. afraid	....	brave
2. small	....	huge
3. throw	toss	....
4. repair	fix	....
5. yell	....	whisper
6. cold	chilly	....
7. difficult	hard	....
8. angry	mad	....
9. remain	stay	....
10. quick	....	slow

My score: $\dfrac{}{10}$

My time: ....
minutes   seconds

Name: .... **Date:** ....

For Questions 1–5, circle the correct homophones in the sentences.

1. Jay ate (for, four) sandwiches (for, four) lunch today!

2. We (rode, road) our bikes on the bumpy (rode, road).

3. The fresh (flower, flour) in her hair was as white as (flower, flour).

4. I (threw, through) the ball (threw, through) the hoop.

5. Tie a tight (knot, not) on the blue rope, (knot, not) the red one.

For Questions 6–10, circle the correct meaning for the underlined homograph in each sentence.

6. The music producer wants to <u>record</u> Jo's songs.
   a. to store sound on disc   **b.** a disc with music on it

7. I would love to see her <u>live</u> in concert some day.
   a. to have life   **b.** a performance in person

8. Jonathan felt <u>well</u> after taking his medicine for a week.
   a. a deep hole in the ground   **b.** in good health

9. The heavy fog <u>rose</u> up from the city streets.
   a. came to the surface   **b.** a sweet-smelling flower

10. Mrs Ross is going to <u>lead</u> us through the parade.
    a. a soft, grey metal   **b.** to show the way

My score: ——
10

My time: ....
minutes   seconds

Name: .... **Date:** ....

Write Yes if the underlined article is used correctly or No if it is not.

1. From the winter to the summer, <u>a</u> weather where I live changes greatly.

   ....

2. Since my mum painted my room, <u>the</u> curtains don't match.

   ....

3. You will need <u>an</u> umbrella that is bigger.

   ....

4. Can you help me clean <u>the</u> shoes that are full of mud?

   ....

5. My favourite singer will be on <u>a</u> radio doing an interview.

   ....

6. <u>An</u> teacher was happy that all of her pupils passed the test.

   ....

7. My report on whales and dolphins won <u>a</u> award.

   ....

8. <u>An</u> anteater walked across the road in front of my car.

   ....

9. <u>The</u> light from the lamp is too bright.

   ....

10. I caught a cold after playing in <u>a</u> rain.

    ....

My score: $\dfrac{\quad\quad}{10}$

My time: ....
minutes   seconds

Name: .... Date: ....

Write the correct preposition to complete each sentence.

1. I sat .... Lisa and Jennifer at the theatre.
   between   off

2. The girls fought .... which one should go first.
   off   over

3. The ambulance arrived .... a few minutes.
   within   above

4. I sat .... the tree for some shade.
   under   over

5. It began to rain ....we got home.
   after   near

6. Please put the plate .... the fork.
   beside   within

7. Gary is .... Melbourne, Australia.
   before   from

8. I finally fell asleep .... midnight.
   toward   around

9. Sarah and Mick sit .... me in class.
   near   within

10. Angus left home .... his homework.
    without   within

My score: ___
          10

My time: ....
            minutes   seconds

Minute 89

Name: .... Date: ....

Write Yes *if the sentence ends with the correct punctuation or No *if it does not.

1. Dana made a pecan pie with her mother? ....

2. Rachel's hair was soaking wet after the rain. ....

3. Frank and Paula fought over washing the dishes. ....

4. Wow, those race cars are going fast! ....

5. We baked oatmeal raisin cookies for the class party! ....

6. The thunderstorm yesterday lasted for two hours. ....

7. Richard shovelled the sand off of the footpath? ....

8. When are we going to announce the winners? ....

9. Cameron is on her way to school now! ....

10. My mother gave me medicine for my fever. ....

My score: $\frac{}{10}$

My time: ....
minutes   seconds

Minute 90

Name: .... **Date:** ....

Insert the missing commas in the sentences.

1. I'll never forget what happened in Madrid Spain.

2. Jess Aymee and Em are three sisters.

3. Mark lives at 78 Chester Street, Plymouth Devon.

4. The walls in my room are painted pink brown and white.

5. I have travelled to Italy France Germany and Spain.

6. In 2008 46 069 people visited Antarctica.

7. Instead of eight six buns should be bought.

8. Uncle Keith lives in Aberdeen Scotland.

9. Paul plays piano violin and drums.

10. Our new address is 132 Willow Lane Camden London.

My score:

$\dfrac{}{10}$

My time:

....
minutes   seconds

Minute 91

Name: .... **Date:** ....

*Write **N** if the sentence is missing a noun or **V** if it is missing a verb.*

1. .... is studying hard for his science test. ....

2. Rob .... every day at his local library. ....

3. The .... is going to be on plants and animals. ....

4. The car that zoomed by almost .... me. ....

5. Let's buy a bucket of .... at the cinema. ....

6. .... looked at the stars through a telescope. ....

7. The girls .... each other's nails bright pink. ....

8. My dad always .... the car in the driveway. ....

9. Tony's .... got a flat tyre after he rode over a nail. ....

10. Helen and .... go horse riding often. ....

My score:

$$\frac{}{10}$$

My time: ....
minutes   seconds

Minute 92

Name: .... **Date:** ....

Circle the incorrect word in each sentence, then rewrite it correctly on the line.

1. There are five puppys in the basket. ....

2. Susies dress got dirty at the party. ....

3. Stephanie are a great cook. ....

4. The boys is practising their song. ....

5. Are we driving in the write direction? ....

6. Her ate the fruit in the bowl. ....

7. There are too birds in the nest. ....

8. The rain comed down hard. ....

9. Them are going to the parade today. ....

10. Us will go to the shops after school. ....

My score: $\dfrac{}{10}$

My time: ....
minutes   seconds

Name: .... **Date:** ....

Read the story and circle the 10 words that are incorrect. Rewrite them correctly on the lines.

Bobby have a nice holiday last summer. Him play football with his three best friend. He visited his Aunt helen in york for too weeks. Bobby goed to the beach with his parents and sister. He also red many good books that he hadn't read before. He was glad when school started again so he could told his friends about his fun summer holidays!

1. ....

2. ....

3. ....

4. ....

5. ....

6. ....

7. ....

8. ....

9. ....

10. ....

My score: $\dfrac{}{10}$

My time: ....
                        minutes   seconds

Minute 94

Name: .... Date: ....

Write the correct verb in each sentence.

1. Jaime ....with his toy cars in his room.

play   plays

2. Steve and Jeremy have ....their project already.

finishes   finished

3. The kittens all ....to sleep on the bed.

loves   love

4. The children ....a lot of presents this year.

gets   got

5. The candle is ....brightly on the dinner table.

burns   burning

6. Patty ....tomatoes and carrots for her mum.

chopping   chopped

7. Mrs Harvey ....science every year.

teaches   teach

8. The audience ....when the show was over.

claps   clapped

9. Justine has ....flowers for her teacher.

picked   picking

10. The boys are .... around the mountain tomorrow morning.

hike   hiking

My score: $\frac{}{10}$

My time: ....
minutes   seconds

Minute 95

Name: .... **Date:** ....

Circle the incorrect word in each sentence, then rewrite it correctly on the line.

1. Jenny softly brushed she doll's hair.

   ....

2. The frog jumpd into the pond.

   ....

3. The baby crawled on the floor too his bottle.

   ....

4. Tom basketball game is this Friday night.

   ....

5. Sarah's tooth falled out during lunch.

   ....

6. Mr Rivera read the story to him class.

   ....

7. Closed the door on your way out.

   ....

8. The bird flyed to the nest with a worm.

   ....

9. Charles ride his bike for an hour yesterday.

   ....

10. The three childs play with their toys.

    ....

My score: ___
10

My time: ....
minutes   seconds

Minute 96

Name: .... Date: ....

For Questions 1–5, write C if the sentence is complete or I if it is incomplete.

1. My birthday wish this year. ....

2. His favourite sport is football. ....

3. Amanda and I at the park. ....

4. Went to the shop after school. ....

5. Darby read five books this summer. ....

For Questions 6–10, rewrite each sentence correctly on the line.

6. Their are three computers in our's classroom.

....

7. Tiffany and Noah right stories in his journals.

....

8. The tall trees is blocking the bright son.

....

9. Shawn book is on an shelf over they're.

....

10. Their will be an party at don's house later.

....

My score: $\dfrac{}{10}$

My time: ....
minutes   seconds

Name: .... **Date:** ....

Insert the missing punctuation marks in each sentence.

1. Oscar Amy Christy and Jasmine are in the same class

2. Jason was born on 10 December 1989 in Chicago USA

3. Will you wash the dishes for me tonight

4. We ordered a pizza two salads and garlic bread for dinner

5. That magician can really do some amazing tricks

6. Remember to bathe feed and walk the dog while we are gone

7. Would you like to watch football hockey or netball

8. Wow, I can't believe I just won the big race

9. Marlon visited his grandparents in Malaga Spain

10. Mr Davis teaches maths English science and history

My score: $\frac{}{10}$

My time: ....
minutes   seconds

Name: .... **Date:** ....

Circle the words that need to be capitalised in each sentence.

1. we have to be quiet at peachtree library.

2. holly and chas played together on sunday.

3. my birthday party will be on wednesday.

4. mrs anderson was my first teacher at caroline Chisholm Primary School.

5. My favourite book is *the twits* by Roald dahl.

6. We want to go to burger hut for lunch today.

7. nia and nina swanson are twins.

8. bobby and I went to seal beach on saturday.

9. aunt peggy and uncle joe live on a farm.

10. we had a big easter party last april.

My score: ──── **My time:** ....
10   minutes   seconds

Minute 99

Name: .... **Date:** ....

Circle the incorrect word in each sentence, then rewrite it correctly on the line.

1. Lucy wheres her sandals to the beach.

   ....

2. Leah's hat blue off of her head.

   ....

3. Grant are swimming in his family's pool.

   ....

4. I bought perfume in the sail for my mother.

   ....

5. Lisa and Pam eated dinner with us.

   ....

6. We had hot chips for an snack.

   ....

7. The park were closed when we got there.

   ....

8. This summer, Christy will go two India.

   ....

9. Frank go to see the doctor every year.

   ....

10. Robin little sister just turned five years old.

    ....

My score: ——
                10

My time: ....
              minutes   seconds

Minute 100

Name: .... **Date:** ....

Write the correct word to complete each sentence.

1. Nancy .... opened her birthday present.
   happily   happy

2. Please use a 1–metre ruler to .... the tub.
   measure   measured

3. Polly .... to the finish line and won first place.
   sprinted   sprinting

4. Children under 11 are not .... on the roller coaster.
   aloud   allowed

5. The .... built an ant hill in our garden.
   aunts   ants

6. Luckily, ... grocery store is still open.
   the   an

7. The audience .... excited when the play started.
   were   was

8. We really .... stay up late.
   shouldn't   haven't

9. That film was the .... I have ever seen.
   worse   worst

10. Carmen finally .... her book report last night.
    finishes   finished

My score:

$\overline{10}$

My time: ....
              minutes   seconds

www.prim-ed.com   Prim-Ed Publishing®

Minute answer key

Minute 1
1. I
2. C
3. I
4. I
5. C
6. C
7. I
8. C
9. C
10. I

Minute 2
1. Yes
2. No
3. No
4. Yes
5. Yes
6. Yes
7. Yes
8. We have to be quiet in the library.
9. The pupils are writing letters.
10. I am reading about Christopher Columbus.

Minute 3
1. Dinner
2. My family
3. My brother
4. Roasted pork belly
5. Apple pie
6. My parents
7. The dishes
8. Mum and Dad
9. Rick and the dog
10. I

Minute 4
1. bought a gift for the party
2. blew my scarf away
3. did not see the deer
4. runs six kilometres every morning
5. went to the theatre
6. made a sundae with vanilla ice-cream
7. put the nuts in its mouth
8. is excited about getting a car
9. go hiking at Spring Park
10. works on his science project at the library

Minute 5
1. Rachel
2. Melinda and Claudia
3. Mrs Lee's party
4. My mother
5. My friend, Ashley,
6. am taking guitar lessons from Mr Verlaine.
7. had a piñata at his birthday party.
8. was chirping outside my window.

9. was excited to go skateboarding with his friends.
10. felt sick after eating three hamburgers.

Minute 6
1. Yes
2. Yes
3. No
4. Yes
5. No
6. No
7. Yes

Following answers will vary.
8. My name is . . . .
9. I live in . . . .
10. I am . . . . years old.

Minute 7
1. Yes
2. No
3. Yes
4. Yes
5. Yes
6. No
7. a
8. b
9. b
10. a

Minute 8
1. Yes
2. Yes
3. No
4. Yes
5. Yes
6. No
7. No
8. Yes
9. No
10. Yes

Minute 9
1. Yes
2. No
3. Yes
4. No
5. Yes
6. No
7. C
8. C
9. S
10. S

Minute 10
1. ?
2. .
3. .
4. .
5. !
6. ?
7. .
8. !
9. ?
10. .

Minute 11
1. I
2. C

3. C
4. C
5. I
6. I
7. a
8. b
9. b
10. a

Minute 12
1. a
2. b
3. a
4. a
5. b
6. b
7. a
8. Thomas is a good team leader.
9. I got milk at the market.
10. Jim broke his arm playing football.

Minute 13
1. S
2. P
3. P
4. S
5. S
6. S
7. P
8. P
9. S
10. S

Minute 14
1. C
2. Q
3. E
4. C
5. S
6. Q
7. S
8. C
9. S
10. E

Minute 15
1. .
2. ?
3. !
4. ?
5. .
6. !
7. .
8. .
9. !
10. ?

Minute 16
Order of answers may vary.
1. firefighter
2. teacher
3. Matt
4. school
5. Sydney Opera House
6. playground
7. notebook
8. basketball
9. computer
10. pillow

Minute 17
1. Mary, city
2. Ms Chow, bread
3. blanket, picnic
4. skin, sun
5. Dr Seuss, author
6. twins, costumes
7. boys, cars
8. Doris, glasses
9. bookstore, magazines
10. horses, field

Minute 18
1. No
2. Yes
3. No
4. Yes
5. Yes
6. No
7. country, city
8. girl, woman
9. bunny, deer
10. street, lane

Minute 19
1. Dr Thomas
2. Saturday
3. Mt Everest
4. Prince Harry
5. Waterford
6. Halloween
7. December
8. India
9. Mothering Sunday
10. Ocean Land

Minute 20
1. Jerry, Christmas
2. Stone Mountain
3. Marcia, Monday
4. Peaches, Dr Sam
5. Hansel and Gretel
6. Rick's Steakhouse
7. Stuart Little, EB White
8. Janice, Snowdonia National Park
9. July, Australia
10. Grand Canyon

Minute 21
Order of answers may vary.
1. Harry Potter
2. Dr Smith
3. Aunt Becky
4. Saturn
5. Australia
6. Boggs Primary
7. lemonade
8. microwave
9. pineapple
10. guitar

Minute 22
Order of answers may vary.
1. doll
2. birthday
3. country
4. room
5. present
6. Aunt Gloria

Minute answer key

7. May
8. Asia
9. Ming
10. Elaine

Minute 23
1. They
2. He
3. We
4. She
5. It
6. He
7. She
8. They
9. We
10. It

Minute 24
1. us
2. me
3. them
4. him
5. her
6. them
7. us
8. him
9. It
10. us

Minute 25
1. my
2. her
3. his
4. its
5. His
6. Your
7. their
8. its
9. our
10. my

Minute 26
1. his
2. your
3. my
4. her
5. their
6. her
7. my
8. its
9. our
10. his

Minute 27
Order of answers may vary.
1. Dr Watson
2. nurse
3. librarian
4. hospital
5. library
6. office
7. medicine
8. blanket
9. book
10. table

Minute 28
1. common noun: planes
   proper noun: Frank
2. common noun: jumpers
   proper noun: Barbara

3. common noun: bunny
   proper noun: Cindy
4. common noun: park
   proper noun: Judy
5. common noun: sister
   proper noun: Oxford
   University
6. common noun: boats
   proper noun: Lake Grace
7. common noun: class
   proper noun: William
   Shakespeare
8. common noun: man
   proper noun: Norway
9. common noun: birthday
   proper noun: November
10. common noun: home
    proper noun: Eve

Minute 29
1. They
2. them
3. He
4. We
5. her
6. We
7. She
8. us
9. him
10. They

Minute 30
1. her
2. my
3. our
4. his
5. their
6. its
7. his
8. her
9. their
10. its

Minute 31
1. babies
2. classes
3. ropes
4. computers
5. trumpets
6. porches
7. boxes
8. ladies
9. kittens
10. cities

Minute 32
1. matches
2. stories
3. pencils
4. foxes
5. peaches
6. owls
7. animals
8. cherries
9. pupils
10. butterflies

Minute 33
1. singular: dog
   plural: owners
2. singular: table
   plural: candles

3. singular: bird
   plural: worms
4. singular: bucket
   plural: umbrellas
5. singular: neighbour
   plural: poodles
6. singular: zoo
   plural: zebras
7. singular: box
   plural: glasses
8. singular: guitar
   plural: strings
9. singular: car
   plural: friends
10. singular: girl
    plural: seashells

Minute 34
1. stickers
2. belt
3. farmer
4. scarves
5. game
6. windows
7. oranges
8. socks
9. duck
10. pizza

Minute 35
1. wolves
2. feet
3. teeth
4. children
5. lives
6. men
7. mice
8. shelves
9. geese
10. sheep

Minute 36
1. leaves
2. elves
3. people
4. women
5. oxen
6. mice
7. feet
8. calves
9. children
10. knives

Minute 37
1. Jason's
2. horse's
3. Mona's
4. elephant's
5. Tom's
6. girl's
7. Wendy's
8. team's
9. sister's
10. Yesterday's

Minute 38
1. girls'
2. grandparents'
3. pupils'
4. brothers'
5. friends'

6. firefighters'
7. kids'
8. dogs'
9. classes'
10. birds'

Minute 39
1. army
2. pair
3. herd
4. pack
5. galaxy
6. chorus
7. crowd
8. stack
9. pile
10. swarm

Minute 40
1. stack
2. team
3. crew
4. deck
5. flock
6. family
7. cast
8. fleet
9. litter
10. bundle

Minute 41
1. buddies
2. faces
3. classes
4. toys
5. pianos
6. days
7. prizes
8. bunnies
9. foxes
10. computers

Minute 42
1. whiskers
2. cakes
3. centimetres
4. friend
5. waves
6. computer
7. coins
8. dress
9. turkeys
10. tomatoes

Minute 43
1. calves
2. deer
3. children
4. wives
5. potatoes
6. teeth
7. torpedoes
8. loaves
9. sheep
10. women

Minute 44
1. cat's; S
2. house's; S
3. pupils'; P
4. Elaine's; S

Minute answer key

5. Ali's; S
6. classes'; P
7. Lindsey's; S
8. birds'; P
9. cup's; S
10. Trevor's; S

Minute 45

1. audience
2. couple
3. cluster
4. collection
5. colony
6. mob
7. portfolio
8. squad
9. school
10. team

Minute 46

1. waved
2. chirped
3. take
4. wanted
5. knead
6. rolled
7. rested
8. shuffle
9. ran
10. sneezed

Minute 47

1. sweep
2. growl
3. squeak
4. scare
5. read
6. sprint
7. mumble
8. wink
9. grow
10. prance

Minute 48

1. sharpened
2. surprised
3. howled
4. whispering
5. celebrate
6. talked
7. cried
8. watches
9. yells
10. rested

Minute 49

1. shouts, shouted
2. honks, honked
3. blink, blinked
4. smile, smiled
5. gallops, galloped
6. hope, hoped
7. snores, snored
8. sniffs, sniffed
9. ask, asked
10. bakes, baked

Minute 50

1. am
2. are
3. was
4. is
5. were
6. is
7. are
8. am
9. was
10. were

Minute 51

1. is
2. am
3. were
4. is
5. are
6. were
7. was
8. is
9. am
10. were

Minute 52

1. have
2. is
3. are
4. has
5. was
6. were
7. has
8. am
9. have
10. were

Minute 53

1. No
2. Yes
3. Yes
4. No
5. Yes
6. Yes
7. No
8. Yes
9. Yes
10. Yes

Minute 54

1. swept
2. bit
3. took
4. built
5. fed
6. driven
7. forgotten
8. froze
9. wore
10. hung

Minute 55

1. blew
2. chose
3. drove
4. drank
5. eaten
6. flew
7. forgot
8. given
9. rang
10. written

Minute 56

1. grills
2. clapped
3. hike
4. play
5. followed
6. teaches
7. changed
8. enjoyed
9. rips
10. giggled

Minute 57

1. reached
2. scared
3. bakes
4. barked
5. snores
6. smiles
7. bounced
8. growls
9. kicked
10. watched

Minute 58

1. are
2. am
3. was
4. was
5. were
6. is
7. was
8. were
9. am
10. is

Minute 59

1. helping: have
   main: sent
2. helping: has
   main: skateboarded
3. helping: is
   main: walking
4. helping: am
   main: putting
5. helping: have
   main: taken
6. helping: has
   main: been
7. helping: is
   main: building
8. helping: are
   main: listening
9. helping: has
   main: lived
10. helping: is
    main: waiting

Minute 60

1. did
2. was
3. forgiven
4. sworn
5. rode
6. flown
7. threw
8. been
9. grew
10. spoken

Minute 61

1. blue
2. smooth
3. pink
4. five
5. strong
6. fruity
7. sick
8. great
9. gloomy
10. white

Minute 62

1. louder
2. best
3. smallest
4. funnier
5. younger
6. noisiest
7. latest
8. earlier
9. wisest
10. longer

Minute 63

1. happily; how
2. shyly; how
3. downstairs; where
4. tomorrow; when
5. quickly; how
6. outside; where
7. meanly; how
8. daily; when
9. proudly; how
10. everywhere; where

Minute 63

1. happily; how
2. shyly; how
3. downstairs; where
4. tomorrow; when
5. quickly; how
6. outside; where
7. meanly; how
8. daily; when
9. proudly; how
10. everywhere; where

Minute 64

1. inside
2. sadly
3. often
4. near
5. proudly
6. far
7. carefully
8. under
9. Sometimes
10. loudly

Minute 65

1. popcorn
2. bookshelf
3. homework
4. sunlight
5. blackbird
6. notebook
7. shoelace
8. skateboard
9. snowflakes
10. headache

Minute answer key

Minute 66
Order of answers may vary.
1. sweetheart
2. starfish
3. tablecloth
4. toenail
5. sunset
6. spacecraft
7. sunflower
8. pancake
9. driveway
10. rainbow

Minute 67
1. No
2. No
3. Yes
4. Yes
5. No
6. No
7. Yes
8. Yes
9. Yes
10. No

Minute 68
1. Mark, Veronica
2. Maths, history
3. sunny, cloudy,
4. mushrooms, bacon,
5. Sunday, Monday
6. Bristol, Bath
7. hat, scarf
8. *Animalia*, *The giving tree*
9. nature, history
10. characters, setting

Minute 69
1. can not
2. I am
3. I have
4. are not
5. you will
6. it is
7. she is
8. will not
9. you are
10. does not

Minute 70
1. they're
2. he's
3. don't
4. we've
5. wasn't
6. you'd
7. what's
8. isn't
9. shouldn't
10. she'll

Minute 71
1. fastest
2. lavender
3. yellow
4. nicer
5. juicy
6. dirty
7. cold
8. brisk

9. funnier
10. brightest

Minute 72
1. inside
2. slowly
3. late
4. happily
5. outside
6. today
7. quickly
8. busily
9. down
10. daily

Minute 73
1. footpath
2. barnyard
3. football
4. butterfly
5. sailboat
6. sunrise
7. tablecloth
8. rainbow
9. textbook
10. doorknob

Minute 74
1. tent, sleeping bag
2. By 2010, 23
3. Ben, Sarah
4. Christchurch, New Zealand
5. film, *The goonies*,
6. purple, pink,
7. roller coaster, Ferris wheel
8. books, wrote
9. chicken, potatoes
10. Edinburgh, Scotland

Minute 75
1. I've
2. didn't
3. we'll
4. aren't
5. he's
6. shouldn't; should not
7. you're; you are
8. I'll; I will
9. can't; can not
10. hasn't; has not

Minute 76
1. incorrect
2. impossible
3. rewind
4. preplan
5. triangle
6. unable
7. uniform
8. nonstop
9. disagree
10. biplane

Minute 77
1. painter
2. broken
3. hopeful
4. happily
5. friendship
6. useless

7. quickest
8. kindness
9. selfish
10. comfortable

Minute 78
1. Yes
2. Yes
3. No
4. Yes
5. No
6. Yes
7. No
8. No
9. Yes
10. No

Minute 79
1. straight
2. disappear
3. positive
4. blame
5. arrive
6. ugly
7. noisy
8. rude
9. major
10. shallow

Minute 80
1. bear
2. blue
3. piece
4. write
5. wood
6. dew
7. new
8. sew
9. aloud
10. weather

Minute 81
1. a
2. a
3. b
4. b
5. a
6. b
7. c
8. d
9. b
10. a

Minute 82
1. the
2. The
3. a
4. the
5. An
6. a
7. the
8. an
9. The
10. a

Minute 83
1. for
2. off
3. during
4. until
5. with

6. between
7. by
8. over
9. outside
10. upon

Minute 84
1. dis; P
2. bi; P
3. less; S
4. un; P
5. ness; S
6. er; S
7. pre; P
8. est; S
9. ly; S
10. re; P

Minute 85
Answers will vary. Sample answers include:
1. scared or frightened
2. little or tiny
3. catch or grab
4. break or damage
5. scream or shout
6. hot or warm
7. easy
8. happy or joyful
9. leave or depart
10. fast or rapid

Minute 86
1. four, for
2. rode, road
3. flower, flour
4. threw, through
5. knot, not
6. a
7. b
8. b
9. a
10. b

Minute 87
1. No
2. Yes
3. Yes
4. Yes
5. No
6. No
7. No
8. Yes
9. Yes
10. No

Minute 88
1. between
2. over
3. within
4. under
5. after
6. beside
7. from
8. around
9. near
10. without

Prim-Ed Publishing® www.prim-ed.com

Minute answer key

Minute 89
1. No
2. Yes
3. Yes
4. Yes
5. No
6. Yes
7. No
8. Yes
9. No
10. Yes

Minute 90
1. Madrid, Spain
2. Jess, Aymee
3. Plymouth,
4. pink, brown
5. Italy, France,
6. 2008, 46 069
7. eight, six
8. Aberdeen, Scotland
9. piano, violin
10. Lane, Camden

Minute 91
1. N
2. V
3. N
4. V
5. N
6. N
7. V
8. V
9. N
10. N

Minute 92
1. puppies
2. Susie's
3. is
4. are
5. right
6. She/He
7. two
8. came
9. They
10. We

Minute 93
1. had
2. He
3. played
4. friends
5. Helen
6. Adelaide
7. York
8. went
9. read
10. tell

Minute 94
1. plays
2. finished
3. love
4. got
5. burning
6. chopped
7. teaches

8. clapped
9. picked
10. hiking

Minute 95
1. her
2. jumped
3. to
4. Tom's
5. fell
6. his
7. Close
8. flew
9. rode
10. children

Minute 96
1. I
2. C
3. I
4. I
5. C
6. There are three computers in our classroom.
7. Tiffany and Noah write stories in their journals.
8. The tall trees are blocking the bright sun.
9. Shawn's book is on the shelf over there.
10. There will be a party at Don's house later.

Minute 97
1. Oscar, Amy, Christy and Jasmine are in the same class.
2. Jason was born on 10 December 1989 in Chicago, USA.
3. Will you wash the dishes for me tonight?
4. We ordered a pizza, two salads and garlic bread for dinner.
5. That magician can really do some amazing tricks!
6. Remember to bathe, feed, and walk the dog while we are gone.
7. Would you like to watch football, hockey or netball?
8. Wow, I can't believe I just won the big race!
9. Marlon visited his grandparents in Malaga, Spain.
10. Mr Davis teaches maths, English, science and history.

Minute 98
1. We, Peachtree Library
2. Holly, Chas, Sunday
3. My, Wednesday
4. Mrs Anderson, Caroline
5. *The Twits*, Dahl
6. Burger Hut
7. Nia, Nina Swanson

8. Bobby, Seal Beach, Saturday
9. Aunt Peggy, Uncle Joe
10. We, Easter, April

Minute 99
1. wears
2. blew
3. is
4. sale
5. ate
6. a
7. was
8. to
9. goes
10. Robin's

Minute 100
1. happily
2. measure
3. sprinted
4. allowed
5. ants
6. the
7. was
8. shouldn't
9. worst
10. finished